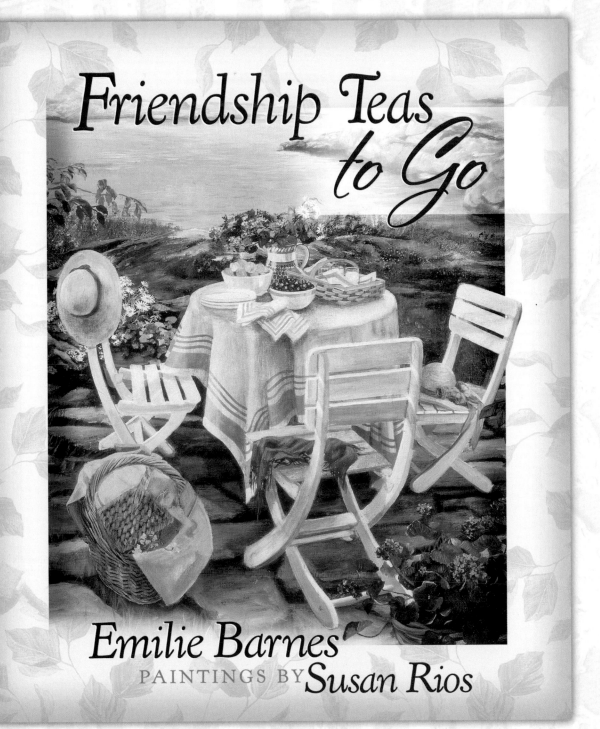

Friendship Teas to Go

Emilie Barnes

PAINTINGS BY Susan Rios

HARVEST HOUSE PUBLISHERS

EUGENE, OREGON

Friendship Teas to Go
Text copyright © 2006 by Emilie Barnes
Eugene, OR 97402

ISBN-13: 978-0-7369-1628-8
ISBN-10: 0-7369-1628-8

For more information about Emilie Barnes, please send a self-addressed, stamped envelope to:

> More Hours In My Day
> 2150 Whitestone Drive
> Riverside, CA 92506

Original Artwork © Susan Rios. For more information regarding artwork featured in this book, please contact Susan Rios, Inc., (818) 995-7467 or www.susanriosinc.com.

Design and production by Garborg Design Works, Minneapolis, Minnesota

Scripture quotations are from the HOLY BIBLE, NEW INTERNATIONAL VERSION®. NIV®. Copyright © 1973, 1978, 1984 by the International Bible Society. Used by permission of Zondervan. All rights reserved.

Printed in China

06 07 08 09 10 11 12 / IM / 7 6 5 4 3 2

Contents

Teatime Anytime!

You don't need much. Don't get caught up in making the gift of tea so difficult, so involved, that you only enjoy it on rare occasions.

Teas to go allow you to redefine the boundaries of formal tea traditions. Unfortunately, stuffy misconceptions have placed limits on sharing the wonders of tea with another or even for yourself.

In my life, I have had many transitions—and the joy of tea goes with me. During the rockiest hardships and the smoothest changes, I sip from the wonderful cup of tea, fellowship, and life.

Tea allows us to enjoy the calm of fellowship, the exchange of communication, and the beauty of taking time for people. Teacups themselves bring something unique and lovely to our time with others. When I am hosting, I love to offer people the chance to choose a teacup from my collection to use for the afternoon. By the time I have returned from the kitchen, they have selected one that called out to them. I love to ask, "Why did you choose that cup?" With a moment to ponder, they seem to know. Maybe it is the green leaf pattern, the single yellow rose bud in the center, or a sunny bird resting on a delicate limb. There is a reason that cup is special to that person, and their choice translates into a more memorable teatime.

This process of having a neighbor, friend, or even stranger choose a cup allows for the conversation to begin. As a teacup is chosen and the warm delicious beverage is poured into that cup, the heart softens and becomes eager to share.

My mother was smart. She understood this very thing. When I was young and came home from school, I would see the teacups out on the table. I knew we would have tea together. By the second cup of tea, I would warm up and begin sharing about my day. She always had a candle on the table. She also had a jelly jar or a small, glass cream bottle as a vase for a bit of ivy or a single fresh flower.

We didn't have much, but thanks to Mother, we really had an abundance of love and kindness. Those conversations were opportunities for her to know me better and for me to have time with my mother. Life was busy then for her. She was trying to support her family all alone after my dad died. These times were precious.

Tea is a way to be together, even if the words or the relationship is not there. Maybe it is a new relationship or a relationship that has experienced some wear and tear over the years. Tea allows you to be in the same space together and to take in the moment at the same time.

Most of all, tea forges deeper friendships—with neighbors, strangers, family members, old friends, and new. May each of these teas to go inspire you to reach out with the cup of friendship. You don't need advance planning or award-winning baking skills. You simply need to offer someone the gift of yourself and your time—and the tea will do the rest.

Emilie

Country Tea

Transporting tea to the country is a simple pleasure that we would be fortunate to enjoy more often and share with others. Just as we need to change our idea of what tea has to look like, we can alter our view of the country. Your trip to the countryside might be a drive to a state park or to the river's edge in the middle of the city. It might be a neighborhood park or a school playground where swings and jungle gyms share a nature space. It might be your backyard by the arbor.

You will discover many reasons to deliver the goodness of tea to friends, family, and neighbors. One of my most precious memories of a transportable country tea was with a dear friend whose husband was diagnosed with leukemia. When she called with the difficult news, I immediately got to packing. A wicker basket with my good china, a teapot, a thermos with hot water, and some baked goodies were prepared for travel. And I knew just the outdoor spot to take my friend. A country park just outside of town would offer us privacy, beauty, and that wonderful feeling of getting away.

Our time in the country was a chance to share tears, thoughts, prayers, and even silence. The warmth of the tea soothed the hurting places of our hearts. And the uncertainty of the recent news was replaced with the certainty of kindness, love, and friendship. We truly shared a cup of hope that day.

The beauty of the outdoors is a perfect backdrop for tea. The birds provide great background music, the setting inspires us to breathe deeply and relax, the

colors open up our minds and hearts to the gift of God's wonder. You can feel your shoulders release the tensions of the day; you might even catch yourself humming or whistling.

Away from the distractions of everyday responsibilities, material burdens, and the pressure of watching the clock, a tea party surrounded by nature gives us many reasons to relax, look at life differently, and experience the joy of the moment. Even though my country tea with my friend was during a difficult time, we both have such special memories of that tea.

We shared our hearts and lives.

We shared the connection of tea.

Tea to Go

While we tend to pack paper cups and plates and plastic utensils for an outdoor get-together, you can just as easily pack your favorite china cups and silverware. I wrapped my teapot in my large red and white checkered tablecloth for protection. Then when we got to the park, I draped the tablecloth on a nearby picnic table.

Do not be afraid to use your special tea treasures. They are meant to be shared with others, and they are intended to brighten your days with beauty *and* function. Let your favorite tea items serve you well. On the shelf they add splendor to your home; in a basket on the way to the country, they add richness to your life.

Packing Light and Right

Wrap cups in cloth napkins and the teapot in the tablecloth.

Use teabags.

Bring hot water (or iced tea for summer) in a thermos.

Susie's Oatmeal Chocolate Chip Cookies

Your friend will indeed feel special when she bites into one of these divine cookies.

1 cup margarine
1 cup packed brown sugar
1 cup granulated sugar
2 large eggs
1 teaspoon vanilla
1½ cups all-purpose flour
1 teaspoon baking soda
½ teaspoon salt
3 cups uncooked old-fashioned oatmeal
14 ounces chocolate chips

Preheat oven to 375 degrees.

In a large bowl, beat margarine until light. Add sugars and beat until fluffy. Add eggs and vanilla and beat well. Stir in flour, baking soda, and salt. Stir in oatmeal and chocolate chips. Using a small ice cream scoop, drop scoops of batter onto an ungreased cookie sheet.

Bake 10-12 minutes or until cookies are just set. Do not overbake these.

Makes 5 dozen.

Beach Party Tea

When you grow up by the ocean like I did, the feeling of the sea never leaves you. There is something so wonderfully peaceful and assuring about the constant rush of the waves and the cycle of the tides. Yet as soothing as the coast is, it also is a perfect place for celebrations. Color, life, distant sounds, open places, and secluded spaces all beckon us to shift our focus from whatever else is going on and turn toward the power and grace of God's shore.

During a difficult time in my journey through cancer, my husband, Bob, and I had to leave our home of many years and move closer to doctors for my treatments. The loss of leaving the place where we raised our family, embraced our grandchildren, and entertained countless friends was eased by our new home's proximity to the shore. I immediately felt its comfort.

Within days, I noticed how the local families took advantage of the community beach just a short walk from the houses. I could look out the windows of our new house and see children, parents, and grandparents carrying baskets of food and armfuls of candles, blankets, even toys, and marching toward the shore. Bob and I needed no prompting; we soon joined this procession for evening meals. I also found myself transporting my teatime to the shore.

Life offers many blessings and surprises. I received a most wonderful one when six friends from high school decided to start getting together twice a year. After forty-five years of occasional calls or letters, we were all gathering face-to-face and enjoying one another's company. When it was my turn to host, I knew right away that I would escort my friends to our community beach. This is where all of us Long Beach gals would feel most at home.

Oh, to have tea by the sea is a way to get real with friends. Off came our shoes and our worries of the day. We could have been nervous about seeing one another after so much time had passed, but even our pace changed from formal to informal as we walked the short way to the beach. By the time our toes were in the sand, our memories, stories, and laughs were rolling like kites in the coastal winds.

Your tea by the beach comes with many natural decorations. You can use shells to outline a space for your gathering. Bring those great tiki torches or plan for a campfire if it will be dark or cool (or have these purely for ambience). Because I love to share my china cups and teapot, this is what I brought with me to the beach. You might want to pack paper cups and plates.

For seating arrangements, we used those close-to-the-ground beach chairs so we could recline in a circle and keep our toes in that warm sand. I prepared finger food so the eating would be easy and informal like our surroundings.

My dear friends immediately relaxed and, with the sound of the sea as background music, we all felt at home. We may have stepped back in time through the sharing of memories, but we moved forward into a new version of our friendships. This is what tea by the sea can do...transport you to a new place with a view that goes on forever.

To the Beach!

If you think "Fourth of July" as you prepare for your beach tea, you will discover many wonderful ways to decorate, dine, and delight.

Sawhorses with plywood planks on top make a great table.

Drape a red-and-white checkered tablecloth or piece of fabric.

Oil lamps on the table create a warm glow.

Centerpieces are all around you—gather and create seashell formations.

Use new beach pails as bowls for green salad and potato chips.

Adorn your table with red, white, and blue—a perfectly nautical color scheme.

Light the sparklers! Bring an assortment of sizes and colors (have a bucket of water handy to extinguish them).

And bring chocolate, definitely chocolate.

Fruity Iced Tea

For sunny days or days you are praying for sun, this iced tea brings summertime to your party, no matter what time of year. This fruity tea punch can be served with a skewer of tropical fruit or a little umbrella for added flavor and color.

1 cup water

1¾ cups sugar

3 cups freshly brewed strong tea

3 cups orange juice

1 cup lemon juice

2 cups pineapple juice

1 quart club soda or seltzer

ice cubes, preferably made from orange
      or pineapple juice

Boil the water and sugar together for five minutes to make a syrup. Mix the tea and juices together, then stir in the sugar syrup. Cover and chill overnight. When ready to serve, fill glass or cup half full with concentrate, add ice, then top off glass with seltzer or club soda. If you prefer, place the entire recipe in a punch bowl, float an ice ring made from juices, and serve.

Makes about 15 8-ounce glasses or 30 punch cups.

Chocolate Bundt Cake

½ cup sugar

¾ cup water

¾ cup oil

4 eggs

1 16-oz. carton sour cream

1 small package (3.9 oz.) instant
      chocolate pudding

1 box yellow cake mix

1 16-oz. package chocolate chips

Preheat oven to 250 degrees.

In a bowl, mix the sugar, water, and oil. Add the eggs, sour cream, pudding, yellow cake mix, chocolate chips. Pour into greased Bundt pan.

Bake one hour. Cool for an hour and put on a cake plate. Dust with powdered sugar.

Thank You Tea

She was there for you during a difficult time. The two of them showed you the ropes when you were the new person in the office. She is the person who can change your mood in the span of a phone conversation.

The list of special people in your life runs the distance between your birth and your life now. Between then and now people of all shapes and sizes have influenced who you are, where you are, or what you long to be.

Conventional ways to express thanks include letters on pretty stationery, phone calls, or simply saying "thank you" with sincerity.

But what about saying thanks with a tea?

If this can be a surprise to-go tea, all the better. You might need to make arrangements with a person's office, secretary, spouse, or another friend in order to create a surprise. This will allow your friend to relax and enjoy the mini-party without worrying.

Here are just a few ideas:

• Wrap up a special teacup and fill it with chocolates, bath salts, an assortment of teas, or colorful jelly beans, and give with a card that reads, "My cup overflows with the sweetness (or fragrance) of gratitude. Thank you!"

• Place a teacup, teabags, small thermos of hot water, plate of home-made chocolate chip cookies (see recipe on page 9) on a wicker, wooden, or silver tray. Sprinkle it with silver-wrapped chocolate

kisses. Present this to your friend with a silver spoon tied with metallic ribbon. The note could read, "You have stirred my heart of thanks with your kindness. Thank you."

- Have the ultimate to-go tea with this fun one. Purchase Chinese take-out boxes and fill them with tea treasures. Use five of them of varying sizes and include the following:
    1. a teacup (ceramic or paper) with a bag of tea
    2. napkins and plastic forks and spoons
    3. tea sandwiches
    4. fortune cookies with homemade fortunes expressing your thanks
    5. chocolate—always chocolate. Place a couple brownies or slices of chocolate cake in the last container.

Place these take-out containers in a large brown paper sack. Then you can either deliver it to the person directly so you can enjoy the tea with her, or you can leave this tea package at a person's door or office as a way to really surprise her. For a note, you can use an inexpensive receipt tablet, such as restaurants use. Tear off a page and write, "You owe me nothing. I owe you everything. Thank you."

If you are in the professional world, this kind of tea package would be a wonderful thank you for a client. If you work as a stay-at-home mom, consider this kind of gesture for a neighbor, babysitter, teacher, or grandparent.

A grateful heart indeed is a cup that overflows. Your desire to celebrate one who has touched your life in some way, big or small, will inspire joy and appreciation in her journey. Saying thank you this way will make an impression on her. She will know how you feel.

Start pouring the cup of gratitude.

Chocolate Cherry Cake

This is simple enough to make the day you want to surprise your thank-you friend. A dollop of whipped cream on top of this with a maraschino cherry really puts this delicious cake over the top!

non-stick cooking spray
1 box chocolate cake mix (enough for
    two layers, with no pudding in mix)
3 eggs, beaten
1 can cherry pie filling
1 teaspoon almond extract
1 cup chopped almonds, divided
1½ cups semisweet chocolate chips
maraschino cherries, drained for garnish

Preheat oven to 350 degrees.

Generously spray a 9 x 13 cake pan with cooking spray and set aside. Empty cake mix into mixing bowl. Add eggs and extract and stir with wooden spoon until well blended. Carefully blend in pie filling and ¾ cup chopped almonds. Pour into prepared pan and bake for 30 minutes or until a toothpick inserted in center comes out clean. When you remove the cake from oven, sprinkle the chocolate chips evenly over the top and cover loosely with a piece of waxed paper. Wait 2 or 3 minutes, then use a metal spatula to smooth the melted chocolate over surface of the cake.

Sprinkle remaining almonds over the top and quickly score the chocolate for serving-sized pieces. Place pan on a wire rack to cool completely before you cut the cake.

Bridal Shower Tea

My daughter, Jenny, recently hosted a bridal shower tea that was spectacular and welcoming. As soon as the women entered her home, they saw colorful, large bunches of helium-filled balloons. And instead of tying theses bunches to chair arms or table legs, Jenny tied the ends to decorative weights so they stayed anchored anywhere she placed them.

These glorious balloon bouquets became a most delightful, transportable decoration. As the guests made their way from the front of the house to another room for the opening of the gifts, Jenny brought the balloons along. Not only did it save time and energy decorating for the gathering, but it added continuity of color and allowed the festive feel to infuse the house.

To create color and mobility for the food, Jenny had a lazy Susan filled with fresh vegetables. She scooped out the red, yellow, and green peppers and used them as "bowls" for a variety of flavored dips. You can also scoop out cabbage or lettuce heads for bowls. At the end of the party, you don't wash dishes—you shred these edible containers and make a salad.

While showers are not an impromptu function like some other teas might be, it is certainly a bon voyage party for the bride-to-be. She is embarking on a new journey—a life and future with a partner. In many ways, her destination is unknown. A shower put on by friends, family members, a church family, or neighbors is a way for people around this woman to support her

May the road rise to meet you,
May the wind be always at your back,
May the sun shine warmly on your face,
The rains fall softly on your fields,
And until we meet again,
May God hold you in the palm of His hand.

IRISH TRAVEL BLESSING

and celebrate the adventure ahead.

I love the idea of creating the party around this journey theme. Available at craft and party supply stores are those fun party poppers that shower streamers in the air—like those used to send off cruise-goers. Decorate the rooms with streamers and flags or fun travel posters. Even maps make interesting and visually stunning wall decorations and tablecloths. If you know the location of the bride's honeymoon, plan the food and décor around this destination. Online or at the library you will find countless books on the cuisine and customs of any location. Have a travel journal as your guestbook to complete the theme.

Carry the warmth of hospitality and generosity through to the close of a shower by ending the time of celebration with a prayer, devotion, or a traveler's blessing. Whisking a bride off to her destination of marriage will be one of the most memorable parties you ever host. As you give the bride much love to take with her, you will be reminded of the many people who have helped you celebrate the transitions, milestones, and paths that have created your own life.

Celebration Carrot Cake

2 cups flour
2 teaspoons baking powder
1½ teaspoons baking soda
2 tablespoons cinnamon
1 teaspoon salt
2 cups sugar
1½ cups canola oil
4 eggs
2 cups grated carrots
1 cup crushed pineapple (drained)
1 cup chopped nuts (pecans or walnuts)

Preheat oven to 350 degrees.

Mix all the above ingredients and pour into a 9 x 13 x 2 pan. Bake for 35-45 minutes or until toothpick comes out clean.

Butter Cream Icing

1 egg yolk
1 cup butter (2 cubes)
8-ounce package cream cheese
1 teaspoon vanilla
1 16-oz. box powdered sugar

Beat together all ingredients until smooth.
Frost cooled cake.
Serve with peach tea or a tea of your choice.

Bridal Shower to Go Ideas

- Send recipe cards in the mail with the shower invitations. Ask guests to write out a favorite recipe and bring it with them to the party. Buy a pretty recipe book or even a photo album with plastic sleeves to place the recipes in. When the bride leaves the party, she will have a cookbook created by the people she loves.

- If the bride and groom will be traveling for their honeymoon, purchase a travel makeup kit and either fill it yourself or ask guests to bring trial sizes versions of the following: toothbrush, toothpaste, deodorant, razor, soap, shampoo, dental floss, lotion, hair clip, lip gloss, sunscreen (if the honeymoon is a sunny location).

- Travel candles are great even when not traveling. Include matches and a few candles.

- Make a video of the bridal shower and have everyone share marriage advice or well wishes. Or a have a guestbook that allows friends and family to jot down their advice. Either way, the bride will have wisdom and encouragement to take with her.

- A great to-go gift (and an excellent group gift) is a picnic basket filled with plastic dishware, non-perishable foods, and of course, tea items.

- If the bride will be moving, fill a small, brown moving box with box labels, nicely designed "I'm moving" cards, a post office change of address packet, a pretty to-do list, stationery, a book of pretty stamps, and packing aids like tape, black markers, and string.

Heart-to-Heart Tea

*E*very time you gather with one friend or more and pour a cup of tea, it is a heart-to-heart experience. Conversation and companionship fill every cup. Fellowship and friendship are served right alongside the cup.

Some very dear women in Mississippi figured out how to have a heart-to-heart tea with me from afar. I first met them while speaking in Mississippi. I'm sure part of my discussion was about my passion for tea. Much later, after I was home and time had passed, I received my diagnosis of cancer. Bob and I decided to post this information on our website to let the friends of our ministry know.

My birthday was approaching, and while I faced it with much hope and faith, I also carried with me thoughts of the cancer's presence in my life for this occasion. One day, I received a package wrapped in brown paper. This was nothing special or different. Our ministry received shipments all the time from business suppliers. But when I tore through the regular postal paper, I knew this *was* something special.

I pared away the brown paper to reveal a beautifully wrapped present. My eyes grew wide, and I'm sure my expression was that of a five-year-old. Isn't it funny how you can have many birthdays in your lifetime and still be giddy about a pretty package? It did my heart wonders just looking at it. I wouldn't even need to open it to receive a blessing.

But I did open it, of course. And inside was the cleverest tea party I have ever seen. These lovely women in Mississippi had arranged a party in a box—decorative paper plates, cups, doilies, an assortment of delicious teas and tea goodies, and the cutest pop-up paper cake complete with candles!

Oh, the joy I felt in that moment! I was consumed with happiness and appreciation for the thoughtfulness of these women I had met once. They taught me something that day. Kindness and friendship rise up to take shape in our lives in surprising ways (like that pop-up cake!). Even miles apart, the spirit of friendship burned brightly, and that is the most important ingredient for a tea party.

Basic Scones

1 cup flour

1 tablespoon baking powder

2 tablespoons sugar

½ teaspoon salt

6 tablespoons butter

½ cup buttermilk

1 egg, lightly beaten

Preheat oven to 425 degrees.

Mix dry ingredients. Cut in 6 tablespoons butter until mixture resembles coarse cornmeal. Make a well in the center and pour in buttermilk. (If you don't have buttermilk, you can use regular milk.) Mix until dough clings together and is a bit sticky; do no overmix. The secret of tender scones is a minimum of handling. Turn out dough onto a floured surface and shape into a 6- to 8-inch round about 1½ inches thick. Quickly cut into pie wedges or use a large biscuit cutter to cut circles.

Place on ungreased cookie sheet, making sure the sides of scones don't touch each other. Brush with egg for a shiny, beautiful golden scone. Bake for 10-20 minutes or until lightly browned.

Lemon Curd

grated peel of 4 lemons

juce of 4 lemons (about 1 cup)

4 eggs, beaten

½ cup butter, cut into small pieces

2 cups sugar

In the top of a large double boiler, combine lemon peel, lemon juice, eggs,

butter, and sugar. Place over simmering water and stir until sugar is dissolved. Continue to cook, stirring occasionally, until thickened and smooth. While still hot, pour into hot, sterilized ½-pint canning jars, leaving about ⅛ inch for headspace. Run a narrow spatula down between lemon curd and side of jar to release air. Top with sterilized lids; firmly screw on bands. Place in a draft-free area to cool and store in a cool, dry place. (I keep mine in the refrigerator.) Lemon curd doesn't keep indefinitely, so make only as much as you will use within a couple of weeks.

Makes about 1 pint.

Heart-to-Heart to Go Idea

Either select a basket or just place the items directly in a box large enough for the following ingredients:

  paper cups
  paper plates with paper doilies on each
  paper, plastic, or fabric tablecloth
  plastic dinnerware
  candles with a book of matches—tie each candle with a
      ribbon for extra color
  scone mix—buy one or make your own by providing the dry ingredients of a recipe and
      writing out the directions for adding the fresh ingredients (you can use the scone
      recipe on page 29)
  tea (choose a selection that suits the occasion)
  a silk flower in a bud vase
  something related to the occasion: a baby rattle, a pretty journal, a carefully wrapped
      teacup, a book on tea, a photo of you

Be creative and personalize your heart-to-heart!

Remembrance Tea

My friend Sheri used to love coffee. She was indifferent, if not completely unexcited, about tea. It just never occurred to her to sip a cup at home. Then she read one of my tea books and realized the offerings of tea—tradition, ritual, refreshment, connection. She could see that all this time she wasn't just missing out on a great beverage, she was missing out on the riches of sharing a freshly brewed pot of tea.

I know since then she has found many ways to incorporate tea into her lifestyle. My absolute favorite idea is her Christmas morning tea with her daughter. Before the household wakes to the scent of breakfast cooking and the joy of Christmas morning, Sheri and her daughter rise, prepare tea, and spend time talking, enjoying the twinkle of tree lights against the dark of the early hour. They look forward to this tradition every season.

This past year, however, Sheri's daughter moved to New York and would not be able to come home for the holidays. So what did they do? They carried on in the tradition of tea (which does not depend at all on geography). On December 25, they each prepared a cup of tea, sat down by their respective phones in their respective homes, and shared their annual Christmas morning conversation. Their tradition now continues in a different shape, form, and style...but the significance is as strong as ever.

It was not much later that Sheri wanted to host a party for her grandmother's ninetieth birthday. And without a second thought, this woman who used to prefer coffee planned a beautiful, memorable tea party. There were five generations of women in attendance at this gathering. Isn't that an incredible image—older women, young women, and girls shared their lives over a cup of tea. It was a chance to bring up memories that had been stored away in time, to cherish the recollections of how their lives intertwined

and interconnected, and to celebrate their beloved grandmother.

Tea does not just complement tradition and times for remembrance—it inspires it. When my group of high school girlfriends first gathered at my house and I served tea, the conversation ended up about my mother. Those women, to this day, remember my mother's tea rituals and her delicious cheesecake. Several of the ladies shared very specific memories of the first time they tried this dessert as young girls. Sweet moments have a way of staying with us forever.

However you choose to celebrate, remember, reminisce, or honor a certain person or life event, invite tea to the party. I guarantee that a touch of tea will make a lasting impression on the guests and on the memories for years to come.

Irene's Cheesecake

*A most memorable dessert from
my mother.*

Crust

> 1 package (¼ box) graham crackers
> 1 stick butter
> ½ cup (2.25 oz.) walnuts or pecans

Put nuts in food processor with blade in
and chop. Put on grater blade to grate
graham crackers and butter. Keep mixing
until evenly blended. Line spring pan with
crust mixture.

Filling

> 4 eggs
> 1 cup sugar
> juice of ½ lemon
> 2 teaspoons vanilla
> 4 8-ounce packages cream cheese

Preheat oven to 350 degrees.

Using food processor, put on grater blade
and put 4 8-ounce packages of cream
cheese through one at a time. Add remaining ingredients. Mix until well blended.
Put in cracker-lined pan and bake for 50
minutes.

Topping

> 2 cups sour cream
> 1 teaspoon vanilla
> ¼ cup sugar

After cheesecake bakes for 50 minutes,
put on topping mixture and bake for an
additional 5-10 minutes.

Make this cheesecake at least one day
ahead. Just before serving, top the cheesecake with cherry or apple pie filling. Or
spoon fresh raspberries over top for a
beautiful and most memorable slice of
cheesecake.

Remembrance Tea to Go Ideas

In Honor of a Person

• Have guests write down a bit of wisdom they learned from the guest of honor—have these read aloud and then gather them to give to the person.

• Many companies create magnets out of photos—have some of these made using a photo of the person being celebrated. Pass these out at the end of the party.

• Create a memory journal. Place a pretty blank book in an area of the room and ask guests to write a brief story, memory, or special thought about the person.

For a Life Celebration (Wedding Anniversary, Birthday, Retirement)

• Gather photos from people of the event or guests of honor. Take these photos to a copy center and have them made into a calendar. Either make one just for the guest of honor or one for every guest.

• If it is a silver or gold wedding anniversary, wrap silver or gold-covered chocolate kisses in tulle and tie with a metallic ribbon.

• Gather music from the era of celebration and make a CD for the evening's entertainment. Give it to the person or couple as a gift.

Neighbors Tea

A year after my bone marrow transplant we were in our new home, and I was so anxious to make my life normal again. In fact, "normal" was the most appealing, exciting, and enticing word imaginable. And normal to me meant having tea with neighbors. But here I was in a new setting, surrounded by people I had yet to meet, so I knew I had to take the initiative.

Christmastime was just around the corner, so I made tea party invitations inviting the women in my neighborhood to come to my home. I dropped one off at each person's house. With the addition of several of my friends, I had quite a crowd of ladies at my place that day. Thankfully, I had prayed and planned for a good response. Teatime necessities like cups, saucers, plates, and silver awaited my guests. Platters and plates with delicious cookies, cakes, and other treats were arranged and displayed with care.

In advance of the special day, I made lots of decorative cookies shaped with clever cookie cutters. There were trees, stars, houses, angels, and crosses—all with touches of colorful frosting, candies, and decorative toppings. They all looked fancy and fun. I asked each woman to select her favorite cookie and then had them return to the living area. I held up the Christmas tree cookie and asked what it was and what went under it.

"Presents," they all responded.

Then I shared about the first and most important Christmas present that was given to us so many years ago. I took time to share my

home and my heart with those around me. The ladies, some of whom did not know each other, soon began to share their own stories. We talked about the neighborhood, our homes, and our holiday traditions.

By the time the tea was over and the last neighbor stepped out my door, I felt like I had truly become close to these ladies. No longer did this seem like a temporary place or a transitional place in my life—this was home. And I was very thankful for each and every neighbor I met that afternoon.

Days later, one of the ladies came by and said, "I'm 82 years old, and I've never been to a tea party. Not only was it my first tea party but it was the most wonderful event I have been to." And I know it was not just the hospitality but it was the heart of faith that was present in that gathering.

I hope you will plan a tea for neighbors of your own. I can honestly say that it changed my experience in my new home and my new life. But even if you don't get around to planning the party, know that if anyone comes over, even without notice, you can have an impromptu tea party. Don't worry about how clean your home is or whether you have your favorite cookies. Being yourself and opening the door wide for someone is the greatest, most heartfelt welcome one neighbor can offer another.

Tea Concentrate for a Group

When you are preparing for a large group tea, you can brew this concentrate up to two hours ahead and still serve hot, perfect tea to your guests. This recipe makes about fifty cups of tea, but you can make more or less concentrate according to your needs. Just remember: To make tea in quantity, don't brew longer—use more tea.

> 1½ cups loose tea or 16 family-size teabags
> 2½ quarts boiling water

Pour boiling water over tea in large non-metallic container such as an earthenware crock. Let steep for five minutes, then strain the tea leaves or remove the teabags.

Store concentrate at room temperature until needed. To serve, use about two tablespoons of concentrate per five-ounce cup—or about three parts of water to every part concentrate. Simply place the desired amount of concentrate in a cup or pot and then add hot water.

Note: This concentrate also makes delicious iced tea. Put four tablespoons in an eight-ounce glass of water, then add water and ice.

To Go Gifts for Guests

• Take fun-shaped cookie cutters and tie them with ribbon. Have each guest select one as a gift before they go. At holiday time, these make pretty tree ornaments—and they are great home decorations anytime of the year.

• Make your own tea gifts. Purchase small tin canisters at a craft or storage store and decorate with wrapping paper or contact paper. Fill each canister with bags of tea or loose tea. Better yet, have this be a craft project to help the women get to know each other.

Welcome
Friends

Tarts and Tea

*A*re you an adventurer?

Have you roamed the world with a friend? Driven across the States with your husband? Climbed the sides of a mountain—just you and a backpack? You might be someone who likes the idea of transporting tea with flair. I like the idea of pairing a theme with teatime, especially if you are spending it with a dear friend who shares your creative spirit or who could use a dose of fun.

A very simple tea to take with you that adds some cultural flair to the moment is a Tart Tea adorned with Scottish tartan plaids. Buy a piece of plaid material at the fabric store. With pinking shears, cut out a large square or rectangle that will be your picnic blanket and then cut out four small squares for napkins.

Wrap silverware and a pie server, tarts or several tartlets, and scones in the napkins. Having scones is essential since they were originally a Scottish quick bread, and they are the ideal complement to tea. Add to your bounty a thermos of hot water, some paper cups, your favorite tea selections, small plastic containers with honey butter and jam, and place all items in the center of the picnic blanket and gather the edges. Tie with a thin twine or, better yet, with a thick plaid ribbon.

Ask your friend to join you at a neighborhood park or even your own backyard. If you are meeting with someone who works downtown, scout out an urban sanctuary like a fountain park or city garden. Along with the beautiful setting, your tarts and tea will also be a delight to the senses. Tarts come in all sizes and with all kinds of fillings. I have friends who adore fruit tarts and others who indulge in only the most chocolate-drenched tartlets. I love them all.

A fun way to sample an assortment is to invite neighbors or friends for a tart-taster party. Each person brings his or her own tart for others to try along with copies of the recipe they use.

Set the table for a formal tea complete with silver teapots and china dishes. Once you arrange the gathering of these tasty treats in your living room or dining room, slice in thin pieces so

everyone can sample each offering. While you serve your perfectly brewed pot of tea, decide as a group who brought the most unique, creative, inspired, or old-fashioned tart. Compile the collection of tart recipes for each person to take with them—along with any leftovers (if there are any!).

Elegant Fruit Tartlets

Make a batch of these elegant petite tarts with a shortbread cookie crust that doesn't require any rolling. Make them with a variety of flavorful fruits—or concentrate on just one that is in season.

1 stick butter, softened

⅓ cup sugar

1¾ cups all-purpose flour

1 cup seedless raspberry jam

1 jar homemade or commercial lemon
   curd

1 pint fresh fruit—blueberries,
   raspberries, strawberries, kiwi,
   peaches

lemon juice, if needed to keep fruit
   from turning brown

Preheat oven to 350 degrees.

Butter miniature muffin pans well or spray with nonstick cooking spray. Cream together butter and sugar until light and fluffy. Add flour and blend until just combined. Roll rounded teaspoons of dough into balls and then press them evenly into bottom and up sides of muffin cups. Use your finger and a cork to work the dough into a tart-shell shape.

Chill shells 15 minutes and then bake in middle of preheated oven for 10-15 minutes or until golden around edges. Let cool 5 minutes and then loosen shells with tip of a sharp knife, transfer to racks, and let cool completely. You can make shells a few days ahead of time and store them in a covered container.

When ready to serve, spread a small amount of raspberry jelly in the bottom of each shell, add a small dollop of lemon curd, and then top with a few pieces of fresh fruit—2 or 3 blueberries, a single raspberry, a wedge of kiwi, a piece of strawberry, or peach slice Toss fruit in lemon juice if the fruit browns easily.

For a delicious variation on this recipe, omit the jam and lemon curd. Arrange the fruit on the tart shells and coat with a glaze of melted apple jelly.

Girdle Scones

You can call these "Scot Pancakes" if you decide to use the tartan theme. The "girdle" in the name actually means "griddle." These traditional Scottish treats are cooked on a griddle or skillet like pancakes but served in a basket, with butter and jam, like regular scones. They make a hardy staple for a family-style high tea.

2 cups flour

¼ teaspoon salt

1 teaspoon cream of tartar

1 teaspoon baking soda

6 tablespoons sugar

1 large egg

1¼ cups buttermilk

2 teaspoons melted butter or oil

Heat a griddle or heavy frying pan and brush lightly with oil or butter. Sift together flour, salt, cream of tartar, and baking soda, then stir in sugar. In a separate bowl, mix egg, butter, and about ¾ cup of the buttermilk. Make a well in center of dry ingredients and add egg mixture, stirring and adding more buttermilk as necessary to make a thick, pancake-like batter. Test the griddle by dropping a small amount of batter onto the surface; bubbles should rise to the top in a few seconds if it is the right temperature.

Drop batter by heaping tablespoons onto hot griddle to make three or four scones. If necessary, spread dough with back of spoon into a flattened, 3-inch round. Cook scones until tops are bubbling and bottoms are brown, then flip with pancake turner to cook other side. Continue with this process until all scones are cooked. You may need to regrease the pan after each batch. As scones are cooked, wrap them in a tea towel or napkin to keep them warm while you cook others. Serve warm with butter and honey or jam.

Princess Tea

*D*id you know that there is a princess in your life? Maybe two, three, even four of them. Perhaps it is you! A princess tea is especially fun to host for your young friends. Not only does it entertain girls, it introduces them to the royal tradition of tea.

Before you even make a guest list, start thinking in rainbow colors, starlight sparkles, and whimsical surroundings. The list of pretty joys is endless:

bubbles—the individual bottles with their own wands for bubble blowing

tiaras—found at most party favor or toy stores and ideal for setting the mood

stickers—lots of shiny stars, cheery flowers, comical bugs...any shape is fun

glitter and face paints—to adorn the adorable faces in attendance

rings and other jewelry—plastic or costume jewelry, the bigger the better

pink and metallic balloons—place these in the driveway and in the eating area

Now that we have the ambience and accessories, we can think about food. Anything with pink is a must. White cupcakes with pink icing topped with jewel candies served on a large silver platter will produce a lot of "ohs" and "ahs" upon presentation. Serve petite cookies like snowballs (recipe on page 49) and pink lemonade or raspberry iced tea.

Emilie's Snowball Cookies

¾ cup shortening

¾ cup butter

1 cup powdered sugar

3 cups flour

½ teaspoon salt

2 tablespoons vanilla

½ cup chopped nuts (any kind will do)

To create a table that meets kingdom beauty codes, scatter pink, yellow, and white confetti sparkles all about. Curl pink and silver ribbon strands and drape them on the chairs, table, even from the light fixtures. I love those round colored pieces of glass that you can find in the home décor sections of stores. Place gold-toned ones in the base of a glass bowl, fill the bowl with water, and then have either floating pink carnations or pink candles in the center.

Preheat oven to 325 degrees.

Cream the shortening, butter, and ½ cup of the powdered sugar together (set aside other ½ of powdered sugar). Sift in the flour and salt and mix. Add in vanilla and nuts for a final round of mixing.

Roll into small balls.

When the girls arrive, keep the party indoors or take it outside. Let the atmosphere be light and fun. There are many ways to entertain with the jewelry, face painting, and bubbles, but when it is close to teatime, set them down and read a story aloud. Then in a whisper, tell the girls that kings and queens and princesses have enjoyed tea throughout the ages, and now it is their turn to carry on this special tradition.

Bake for 20-25 minutes. While still warm, roll the cookies in the remaining powdered sugar. Coat as thick as you like.

After serving, keep remaining cookies in tightly sealed container or freeze. These are great to have on hand any time but especially during the holiday season.

Lilies Tea

My good friend Donna is a fabulous role model. She not only writes about the importance of being a mentor to other women, but she lives this commitment. Once a month, a group of women gather together under her leadership. She calls them her lilies, and they are precious to her. The women, most under the age of 35, have different life situations but find much in common to discuss. They laugh, cry, and grow together as they explore the importance of being friends, daughters, wives, mothers, and even mentors themselves.

I encourage you to open up your life to the possibility of being a mentor. You don't have to be an extrovert, a leader by nature, or a perfect organizer—just as with hosting a tea—all you need is to say yes to hospitality and sharing yourself.

A lilies tea could be your way to initially gather a group of women together. So often we have many different groups of friends or acquaintances—women from work, the neighborhood, church, parent groups, the gym—but we don't usually mix these groups except at big gatherings like weddings or showers. Spend some time considering either a group of younger women you can mentor or a group of peers you want to bring together in the spirit of fellowship and encouragement.

Throughout the year, you can watch for sales and purchase lily or floral themed items: napkins, tablecloths, centerpieces, vases, and invitations. Always list details clearly on an invitation: Who is hosting (your name and phone number), What ("a tea" or even "a lilies tea"), Where (address and directions),

When (day, date, and time). For a first gathering, list the time frame, for example "A tea from 2:00 - 4:00" so that guests understand the possible time commitment.

Greet each woman with a lily and escort her to a table that has a selection of single flower vases. They can then choose their seat at their table by placing their vase and flower by the setting. If they don't know each other, this gives them something to talk about and do as everyone gets settled. Introduce the women to one another and explain how that person is special to you or why you are interested in getting to know this person, "Sally is always so generous with her time at the local fundraisers; I wanted to know more about this kind person."

Other than taper candles, keep your table decorations low so they do not inhibit conversation and the passing of food. Have a light fare of sweets, breads, and tea. Always have coffee or lemon water for those who have not yet learned to adore tea. Allow the conversation to flow naturally. If there are moments of quiet, you can introduce topics such as family, how to stay balanced in a busy world, and the pleasures of tea.

Ask if any of the women would be interested in meeting more regularly. Offer to host the next one to keep the idea simple and feasible for these women. From there, they might want to take turns hosting. But sometimes offering your home on a regular basis is a great blessing to these women who are then able to show up, laugh, talk, and share their lives without the worries of hosting.

Donna's Oatmeal Raisin Cookies

1 cup butter, room temperature
1 cup firmly packed brown sugar
2 eggs
1¼ teaspoon vanilla
1½ cup flour
1 teaspoon baking soda
1 teaspoon cinnamon
½ teaspoon salt
2 ¾ cups uncooked oats
1¼ cup raisins

Preheat oven to 350 degrees.

Cream together butter and sugar; add eggs, vanilla. In separate bowl combine dry ingredients—soda, flour, salt. Add to creamed mixture; add raisins and oats and combine. Drop spoonfuls on cookie sheet and bake for 10-13 minutes depending on your oven. The key to soft, thick cookies is the temperature of the dough when you bake them. For thick cookies, dough should be cool to cold. For thin, flat cookies, dough should be warm and soft.

Just Because You're You Tea

Don't wait for a reason to make some tea and head for your nearest friend. There is no need for her birthday, or for a promotion, or for a big day of any kind. "Just because you're you" is the surefire reason to have a tea. So choose the day, the friend, and get ready to surprise a friend with some time of attention, nurturing, rejoicing. This is especially fun if your friend thinks you are just stopping by to drop off a sweater you borrowed or some other quick-stop reason. When you show up with a picnic basket brimming with a traveling party, she will know she is loved. And what is in that basket will make for an afternoon of celebration—

- chilled bottle of sparking cider
- mint tea bags and a thermos of hot water
- special cups from your collection
- a tin lined with vibrantly colored tissue paper and filled with Confetti Cookies (recipe on page 57)
- a bowl of delicious fruit salad (recipe on page 57)—the coconut looks like confetti
- real confetti in a little plastic bag
- plates, silverware, and cups for tea and plastic flutes for the sparkling cider
- a colorful tablecloth or blanket

Whisk your friend away to a special spot if she has time. Or if she has little ones at home and cannot leave, set up the party in her own living room. Spread the cloth and sprinkle the confetti all around it. Pour the tea or cider and propose a toast, "Because you're you...and you deserve to be celebrated!"

There are many women in your life, including yourself, who deserve this kind of party in the midst of busyness and responsibility and activity—a time to reflect on why they are cherished and special and unique.

Confetti Cookies

These colorful cookies are the perfect way to celebrate a friend.

> nonstick cooking spray
> 1 8-ounce package cream cheese, room temperature
> 2 eggs
> 1 box confetti cake mix
> ½ cup coconut
> ½ cup white chocolate chips

Preheat oven to 350 degrees.

Lightly grease cookie sheets with cooking spray. In a bowl, beat cream cheese and egg together with an electric mixer. Add cake mix, coconut, and white chocolate chips and mix well. Drop by teaspoonfuls onto cookie sheet. Dough will be sticky. If you wish, you can chill for several hours to make it easier to handle. With wet fingers, press down cookies a little and smooth edges.

Bake cookies for 8-10 minutes until edges brown. Allow to cool 1 minute on cookie sheet, then remove to wire racks to cool completely.

Simple Fruit Salad

> 2 15-oz. cans fruit cocktail
> 1 cup sour cream
> 2 bananas
> 1 cup miniature marshmallows
> coconut

Drain fruit cocktail. Mix with sour cream in large bowl and refrigerate. When ready to serve, add sliced bananas and sprinkle with coconut.

Black-and-White Tea

*E*legance can be adorned with a bit of the casual. Fancy can be fanciful and fluid. And by now, we certainly know that tea can be easygoing and inspired. So let's bring our look at "teas that can go any-where" to a close with a touch of class.

When most people consider the idea of hosting a more significant, elegant dinner party, they become overwhelmed. So many details start to surface in one's mind that soon you are rethinking and repackaging your evening plans to look familiar and easy again. Something like take-out pizza!

But a progressive black-and-white party is one you and several friends can be a part of—by hosting and participating. Ideally two or more friends will join you. Spouses will love this as well, so expand the guest list and get ready for a movable feast.

Plan an evening of simple foods that can be elegantly presented. Figure out how

many friends will be participating in this (we will plan for two friends for our example) and divide up the courses any way that works for that count. For example:

- an appetizer with tea at the first house (everyone will gather here first)
- tea sandwiches and/or side dishes at house two
- dessert teas and delights at house three to conclude the evening

The group will meet at the first house and then travel caravan style to the next location and so forth. What I really enjoy about this tea is that you and your friends will make food and décor preparations prior to the start of the afternoon or evening—but then, when you all arrive at your home, your friends can help you make the tea to serve with the appetizer, sandwiches, or dessert. It becomes a very

fun time of community. You can go all out with elaborate details, or keep it quite simple.

Encourage all participants to dress up. How often do we really get to wear floor-length dresses or a basic black dinner dress with a colorful shawl, pearls, and high heels? Not often! Have the men wear suits and ties and, if any children are participating, have them in their Sunday best.

The Appetizer

- If this truly is a ritzy crowd, try serving caviar with white crackers. If your group is not a caviar crowd (mine's not!), then a bowl of black bean dip topped with sour cream and cilantro and served with white corn tortilla chips might feel more appropriate.
- A cheese tray adorned with large, black olives also makes a nice appetizer option.

Tea Sandwiches and Side Dishes

- Prepare a favorite sandwich or some of the tea sandwiches listed on page 62. For a black-and-white tea use a dark rye for half of the sandwiches and a white or sourdough bread for the others. Mix these on the serving platter.

- Bow tie pasta is an easy side dish that can be served hot or cold. No need for heavy sauces, just coat lightly with olive oil, fresh parmesan cheese, and sliced black olives. Mix and serve.
- Have a variety of teas to serve.

Divine Dessert

- Pick out desserts that are easy, fast, and match the color theme, like the Black-and-White Dream Layers on page 62.

For an elegant black-and-white tea, the presentation makes the evening special. Give your guests the luxury treatment by adding unique touches to your part of the evening. Whether it is with music, black-and-white decorations like balloons and

ribbons, or the way you engage them in conversation, make the time together memorable.

An ideal ending for this evening is to take a photo of the group all dressed up. Have black-and-white prints made and, shortly after the day of the party, present each friend or couple with the photo framed in a black or white frame. They will cherish this memento and the evening's memories for years to come.

Traditional Tea Sandwiches

Made from thin bread with crusts removed. Try these fillings:
- thinly sliced chicken breast or smoked salmon with watercress and mayonnaise on white bread

- Stilton cheese crumbled over apples on pumpernickel bread
- cream cheese mixed with chutney, a dash of curry, and lemon juice on white bread
- paper-thin slices of red radish on white bread with unsalted butter
- tomato slices sprinkled with freshly chopped basil on rye bread with mayonnaise

Black-and-White Dream Layers

This dessert has delicious layers that will make your guests want seconds—and the recipe!

1 devils' food cake mix, baked as directed in 9" x 13" pan.
1 small (3.9 oz.) box instant chocolate pudding mix, prepare as directed
8 ounces Cool Whip
3 Heath Bars or Hershey Skor bars

Use half of cake and cut cake into small pieces. Put ½ in bottom of large glass bowl and layer with pudding, Cool Whip, and candy bars. Continue layering, ending with candy bars on top. Chill.